# THE FAMILY
*That Prays Together*
# STAYS TOGETHER

Dear Doris,

I missed you and your gracious presence and beautiful smile at St. Monica's. Along with This book & promise to keep you in prayer especially in Rosary, at Mass & office.

With affection, Fr. Willy

"Through the publication of *The Family That Prays Together Stays Together*, Fr. Willy Raymond brings us an inspiring contemporary guide for turning to the intercession of our Blessed Mother as a means of developing a closer relationship with the Lord. In the midst of the often-challenging circumstances of life, Fr. Raymond calls us to turn to Mary, allowing her to lead us to the comfort, assurance, and peace of her son, Jesus. Building on Fr. Patrick Peyton's foundational work by incorporating St. John Paul II's Luminous Mysteries, Fr. Raymond provides us a source of comfort, strength, and assurance through the Rosary. I hold the daily prayer of the Rosary among the greatest gifts of the Church and encourage all people—younger, older, faith-filled, or seeking faith—to receive the gift of our Blessed Mother's consolation and closeness to Jesus by following Fr. Raymond's very accessible guide. It will bring you untold peace and blessings."

**Cardinal Seán O'Malley**
Archbishop of Boston

"As a young boy, I grew up hearing the phrase 'the family that prays together stays together' uttered by my parents frequently as a precursor to our mealtime or bedtime prayer routine, but I never knew where the slogan came from. The mystery of its origins were ultimately revealed years later, to my delight, in my discovery of Fr. Patrick Peyton through my affiliation with Family Theater Productions. This book is an intimate revelation of Venerable Peyton's powerful devotion to the Rosary, his impact on the world through his love for the Blessed Mother, and her miraculous intercession in his life that started it all, kicking off a prayer revolution that lasted four decades. Fr. Willy Raymond's personal connection to Peyton, his reflections on sacred scripture, and Peyton's life make the venerable priest's love and zeal for this transcendent and history-altering meditation on Christ's life irresistible. Any Christian who wants to exponentially deepen their relationship with Jesus and more fully understand the pivotal role and miraculous power of Mary as intercessor to Our Lord must absolutely read this book."

**Jonathan Roumie**
Actor portraying Jesus in *The Chosen*

"Praying as a family can seem like a daunting task, and when you attempt the Rosary with a young family, it becomes even more daunting. This book makes it so easy for every family to not only know the mechanics of the Rosary but to enter deeply into its mysteries and prayers and to gather their hearts and minds in this tradition. We are thankful for this book and hope many more families will join in this indispensable prayer."

**Deacon Jason and Rachel Bulman**
Contributors to Word on Fire Catholic Ministries

"Fr. Willy Raymond is one of the greatest promotors of the Family Rosary in our contemporary times. Inspired by the spirituality of Venerable Patrick Peyton, Fr. Raymond gently and richly guides the readers on how to pray and reflect on the mysteries of the Rosary, especially in a family context. Everyone, particularly parents, should read *The Family That Prays Together Stays Together*."

**Fr. Fred Jenga, CSC**
President of Holy Cross Family Ministries

# THE FAMILY
## *That Prays Together*
# STAYS TOGETHER

*A Bead-by-Bead Family Guide through the Mysteries*

Discover the Promise and Power of the Rosary with

## FR. PATRICK PEYTON

## FR. WILLY RAYMOND, CSC

AVE MARIA PRESS AVE Notre Dame, Indiana

*Nihil Obstat*: Reverend Monsignor Michael Heintz, PhD
            *Censor Librorum*
*Imprimatur*: Most Reverend Kevin C. Rhoades
            Bishop of Fort Wayne–South Bend
            Given at Fort Wayne, Indiana, 26 August 2023

The *Nihil Obstat* and *Imprimatur* are official declarations that a book or pamphlet is free of doctrinal or moral error. No implication is contained therein that those who have granted the *Nihil Obstat* or *Imprimatur* agree with its contents, opinions, or statements expressed.

The publisher wishes to acknowledge Laetitia Rhatigan for the consolidation of archival citations in her doctoral dissertation "Her Will: The Writings and Works of Servant of God, Patrick J. Peyton, CSC, as They Reflect His Marian Spirituality."

---

Founded in 1865, Ave Maria Press is a ministry of the United States Province of Holy Cross.

www.avemariapress.com

Paperback: ISBN-13 978-1-64680-255-5

E-book: ISBN-13 978-1-64680-256-2

Cover image © www.gettyimages.com.

Interior images: Gettyimages.com 4, 8, 12, 28, 32, 36, 40, 44, 52, 56, 60, 64, 68, 76, 80, 84. Alamy.com 88, 92.

Cover and text design by Katherine Robinson.

Printed and bound in the United States of America.

*Library of Congress Cataloging-in-Publication Data is available.*

Where does prayer fit in today?
I'd say, where does your heart fit in in your body?
Where does the air fit in when you breathe?
It's an essential dimension in our very lives.

—Venerable Patrick Peyton, CSC

# Contents

# Preface

When I was growing up in a small city in Maine, one of twelve children in a Franco-American Catholic family, we prayed the Rosary in French every night in October, during Lent, and in May. The Rosary usually followed dinner, and I vividly recall the voice of my mother slowly reciting the Our Fathers, Hail Marys, Glory Bes, the Litany of the Saints, and acts of contrition, faith, hope, and charity. We children did not always observe this sacred time with exemplary piety, but the prayers ended with the consolation of a few precious but fleeting moments of unity, peace, and joy.

I didn't know it at the time, but my family was part of a global movement for families to pray the Rosary together. The man who sparked and led that movement— the famous "Rosary Priest," Venerable Patrick Peyton— spoke to more people face-to-face than any other human being in history in his time. Millions flocked to his legendary Rosary rallies and left reinvigorated in faith and prayer.

As a fellow religious of Holy Cross, I was privileged to know Fr. Peyton for thirty years. He was a gentle, pious man and faithful priest of Holy Cross. He always had a Rosary wrapped around his right fist and was ever ready to share the reason for his devotion to Blessed Mary and to invite you to pray the Rosary with him. He loved the Grotto at the University of Notre Dame; the great Marian shrines in Brazil, France, Portugal, and Mexico; and Michelangelo's *Pieta* statue in St. Peter's Basilica in Rome. He never lost his lyrical Irish brogue and spoke the name of Mary with obvious relish and affection as only the Irish can.

When reflecting on Pope Paul VI's apostolic exhortation *Marialis Cultus* (*Marian Devotion*), Fr. Peyton wrote, "The rosary is now revealed in a brilliant light for what it is; a precious jewel, a compendium of the gospel, a gospel prayer, a prologue and epilogue of the Eucharistic sacrifice—the Mass, and *one of the greatest and most effective prayers for the family.*" He was overjoyed at its counsel to "look to Mary, call upon Mary, listen to Mary, and hold fast to Mary . . . to take the Rosary into our hearts and homes and through it grow in grace, wisdom, and strength to enable us to cope with life today and [its] overwhelming challenges."[1]

Fr. Peyton knew Mary was real and alive and actively working for our good. This conviction was born of personal experience—Mary literally saved his life. As a young man, he suffered from tuberculosis and was told he would not recover. A Holy Cross priest who was a mentor to the young Patrick Peyton visited him and encouraged him to turn to Mary because Jesus never says no to his mother. The conversation made an impact. Fr. Peyton said, "To a greater extent than ever before, he helped me to realize how human she is, how approachable, how sensitive to our needs, so that she could never be haughty or turn her back when we call her."[2] He decided to put his trust in God and to approach him through Mary.

When he made a miraculous and dramatic recovery, Patrick Peyton dedicated the rest of his life to making Mary known and loved through the Rosary, with a special focus on urging families to pray it in the home. At a talk in Nazareth in 1971, he said, "For this I have come amongst you. . . . thanks be to God, Mary is real for me. She is alive. She is somebody's daughter. She knows what it is to be on this earth of ours. She knows what sorrow is, what fear is, what poverty is, what deprivation and destitution are."[3]

Mary is real for you, too. My hope for this book is that it offers you a way to deepen your relationship with Mary and, in doing so, deepen your relationship with her son, Jesus Christ. And the best way to approach Mary is through the Rosary.

The Holy Rosary is a highway to the riches of the Heart of Christ. To pray the Rosary is to set out on a

journey of grace in which the pilgrim experiences the
joys, the illuminations, the sorrows, and the glories of
God's Son and his holy mother. To our surprise and
delight, the events captured in each mystery of the Rosary
are to be found also in every pilgrim's life. Through rep-
etition, immersion, meditation, and contemplation, the
Church invites each person, each family, each community to travel in prayer in company with the humble maid
of Nazareth. She takes each and all by the hand and leads
us with the confident grace of the Mother of God. In
prayer, the devout pilgrim finds Mary pointing to the
reality that each mystery is lived, not only in the life of
Christ, but also in one's own life.

Before we begin, join me in praying with Fr. Peyton
these words of praise that he captured in a journal entry
in November 1967:

> Dearest and most beloved Mother of God,
> you are indeed extraordinary,
> beloved of God the Father,
> beloved of God the son,
> beloved of God the Holy Ghost,
> beloved of God in His unity,
> beloved of His in his blessed sacrament,
> beloved of men,
> beloved of me.

Oh! Wonderful and blessed and loved and
    beloved Mary.
You are related to me.
Oh most beloved, revered, and honored
    Mother of God, Mary most holy.
How blessed I am to be beloved of Mary,
to be protected by Mary,
to be guarded by Mary,
to be trained by Mary,
to be defended by Mary,
to be honored by Mary,
to be remembered by Mary,
to be disciplined by Mary,
to be a friend of Mary,
to be treated so nobly by Mary,
to be expected by Mary,
to be revered by Mary,
to be looked upon by Mary,
to be loved by Mary,
to be watched over by Mary,
to be saved by Mary,
to be recommended by Mary,
to be loved and believed by Mary,
beloved daughter of God the Father,
beloved Mother of God the Son,
and most beloved Spouse of God the Holy
    Ghost.

How blessed is Mary,
how wonderful is Mary,
how loved is Mary,
how beloved is Mary,
how honored is Mary,
how revered is Mary.[4]

# How to Use This Book

This book will help you walk through a month with Mary at your side. If you pray the Rosary daily, the reflections here will help you cultivate a deeper devotion to our Blessed Mother. If the Rosary is a new devotion, this book will help you step into the rhythm of this prayer and set a firm foundation for it to nourish your spiritual life in years to come. Either way, your companion for this journey is Venerable Patrick Peyton, CSC, one of the greatest advocates for devotion to Mary that the world has ever seen.

This book is particularly well suited for families who want to make the Rosary a part of their shared life of prayer. It introduces the whole Rosary (all four sets of mysteries) over the course of a month, allowing you to ponder together just one decade and mystery a day. It will not tax the attention span of children, and after a month, everyone will have a firm grasp of the rhythm of this prayer. By integrating it into your celebration of Sunday Mass, you will establish a firm spiritual foundation for your family.

Why is a devotion to Mary helpful in the life of Christian discipleship? Mary shares a special union with her son. From his conception through his death on the Cross, Mary was singularly present to Jesus's saving mission and participated in it. From that vantage point, Mary can help us in several ways:

- She prays for us. Fr. Peyton knew she was a powerful intercessor; he turned to her to save his life. He continued to rely upon her prayers in his ministry and witnessed the power of her intercession through the millions of people he reached.

- She is our model of faithfulness. The *Catechism of the Catholic Church* describes Mary as "the masterwork of the mission of the Son and the Spirit" (721). She was specially prepared by God to bear Jesus to the world. As a person who received God's Word and remained faithful to him, she embodies the mission we are called to by virtue of our own baptism.

- She is a sign of hope. When Mary died, she was assumed into heaven, body and soul. Because of her unique role in salvation, she fully participates in Jesus's Resurrection and thus shows us our own destiny when our pilgrimage of faith is over.

Because she was Jesus's mother, Mary is also our mother of grace. She cooperated with God to bring Jesus into the world and continues that work among us today. We can rely upon her for help in our life of faithfulness.

Fr. Peyton certainly did. When he was facing incurable illness, a spiritual advisor visited him and encouraged him to turn to Mary, telling him that God never says no to his mother. As Fr. Peyton recounted in his autobiography, *All for Her*,

> I felt that he was building a bridge for me over the chasm that spelt the difference between theory and reality, that he was leading me across that bridge so that I could see Mary, could walk with her, talk to her, realize that she was a real person who would listen, love, respond. I will not say that I really saw Mary for the first time while he talked, but I know I saw her with a new clarity and intensity, so that I could say in my heart, "Mother, I believe that you are alive, that you are real, that you are a woman, that you have eyes, a face, a smile, a memory, an intelligence, a heart. You have a mother and a father of your own. You have a son, who is truly God, who loves you, who will deny you nothing you ask."[5]

Fr. Peyton was miraculously cured and subsequently dedicated his life to spreading devotion to Mary, especially through the Rosary. He reached millions of people through the power of mass media and the popular Rosary rallies that he regularly hosted. The words and reflections of this holy priest, who moved so many people to a deeper faith, will guide you as you approach Mary in this book.

Fr. Peyton knew that we could trust Mary to bring us to Jesus, and he knew that we could trust the Rosary to bring us to Mary. That's why he never tired of encouraging people to pray the Rosary. (If this is a new devotion for you, see appendix B, "How to Pray the Rosary.") This book is crafted around four weeks to progress through the four movements of the Rosary—the Joyful, Luminous, Sorrowful, and Glorious Mysteries—because they draw us into the life of Jesus through the eyes of his mother.

The goal of this book is to help you establish a habit of daily prayer rooted in devotion to our Blessed Mother. To that end, each day's prayerful reflection is built around the rhythm of the Rosary. As you open this book each day, you'll move through these elements:

- a prompt to begin with the Our Father, just as each decade of the Rosary would begin

- a quote from scripture that anchors the mystery

- a brief reflection that breaks open the mystery, often drawing upon the words and life of Fr. Peyton

- a prompt to recite the Hail Mary ten times, followed by the Glory Be
- a concluding prayer that sends you into the rest of your day with a point of focus

Over the course of the week, you will pray an entire set of mysteries of the Rosary, a decade each day, with the benefit of prolonged contemplation on the life of Jesus and Mary. Seeing these mysteries through the eyes of Fr. Peyton will reveal new dimensions of faith, hope, and love.

Because each set of mysteries of the Rosary holds five decades, you'll have two additional days each week to bring to prayer. A good approach would be to create a regular routine like this:

- Monday through Friday: Pray with each day's entry from this book.
- Saturday: Pray all five mysteries of the Rosary that were the points of focus for the week.
- Sunday: Bring the fruits of your prayer to Mass. This book provides open space at the end of each week's mysteries for you to journal and record your insights, joys, and concerns from the week's prayer.

Whether you are new to the Rosary or have been praying it all your life, this book will help you approach this ancient and well-worn prayer with the enthusiasm and love of one of its greatest advocates. By the end of the month, you will have prayed through all twenty mysteries of the Rosary, which condense scenes from the gospels and help us contemplate the face of Christ through the eyes of Mary, our mother.

Fr. Peyton's famous Rosary rallies lifted the hearts of millions who gathered around the world to hear him speak, and he reached millions more through radio and television. Let his words lift your heart, too. With your prayer guided by his voice, you'll discover new strength and peace in a renewed connection with God.

# The Life of Venerable Patrick Peyton

John and Mary Peyton welcomed their sixth of nine children to the world on January 9, 1909. They raised baby Patrick in a thatch-roofed, two-room cottage on the blustery, rainy west coast of Ireland in County Mayo. Their small subsistence farm did not yield enough produce or revenue to prevent the family from experiencing periodic hunger and chronic poverty. Though the family was materially poor, they were rich in faith. Every night after dinner, Patrick's father would gather the family to pray the Rosary.

When Patrick was a boy, he dreamed of becoming a priest. While his siblings worked the fields, Patrick was allowed to attend school a bit longer so he could prepare for admission to a seminary to study for the priesthood. He applied to many missionary orders of priests but was rejected because he lacked suitable education and funds to pay for seminary.

Saddened by these rejections, he abandoned the dream of priesthood and, when he was nineteen, left home for America with his brother Tom. They both hoped to become millionaires in Scranton, Pennsylvania, but God had other plans for Patrick and his brother. Tom found a job working in coal mines, but no one would hire Patrick. Desperate, he took the one job offered to him as a janitor at St. Peter's Cathedral in Scranton. There, he continued to pray the Rosary every day, just as he had with his family back home.

In the cathedral, often alone at the end of the day, Patrick again felt the tug of God's call to be a priest. When a team of Holy Cross priests from the University of Notre Dame came to lead a mission at the cathedral, Patrick's pastor introduced the two brothers to them as potential future priests in the Congregation. Soon after, Patrick and Tom moved to Notre Dame to enter the Holy Cross seminary there.

Patrick loved the seminary. He felt he was finally on the path to becoming the missionary priest he had always desired to be. One day, however, he became very sick with tuberculosis. The doctors told Patrick that he might never recover. After being ill for an entire year, he took a turn for the worse. His doctors gave him two choices: they could perform a surgery that would make him unable to perform day-to-day tasks for the rest of his life, or he could simply pray for a miracle. They did not have much hope for him.

A priest who had been Patrick's favorite professor at Notre Dame, Fr. Cornelius Hagerty, CSC, told Patrick to pray to Mary, the Mother of God, for her intercession. He told Patrick to ask Mary for a healing, saying that she would bring that prayer directly to God. "Our Lady will be as good as you think she is," Fr. Hagerty said. "If you think she is a fifty per-center, that is what she will be; if you think she is a hundred per-center, she will be for you a hundred per-center."[6]

Patrick put all his trust and faith in the Blessed Mother, and she did not fail him! His friends and family prayed the Rosary with him for his healing, and he was miraculously made well again.

Patrick completed his studies and became a priest. He spent the rest of his life encouraging families to pray together because family prayer—especially the Rosary— is the greatest force for good in heaven or on earth. He always told people that "the family that prays together stays together."

In 1942, as the world was at war, Fr. Peyton organized groups of families to pray the Rosary together. He called his organization the Family Rosary Crusade. He challenged them to pray the Rosary daily, assuring them that "a world at prayer is a world at peace." He traveled to countries all around the world telling people about the family Rosary as a powerful tool in their hands.

Fr. Peyton faced many challenges but always prayed his Rosary—and amazing things happened. Through this work, he became the missionary priest he had always dreamed of being. He spoke live, in person, to more than 28 million people at Rosary rallies on six continents. At the time (before computers and the internet), it was the largest number of people any one person had ever addressed. Some rallies (in Brazil and the Philippines) had two million people in attendance—all to hear this Irish priest speak of the love of Mary for each of them and the power of the Rosary to draw them closer to Our Lord and each other.

Fr. Peyton went to Hollywood to invite well-known actors to pray the Rosary with him on radio and television. He wanted to use all means possible to spread his message of family prayer—especially the family Rosary. Many famous people of that time did help him, and in 1947, he founded Family Theater Productions based in Hollywood, a ministry that is still using the power of media to bring Fr. Peyton's message to the world.

Fr. Peyton died early in the morning on June 3, 1992, at the age of eighty-three. His final words were, "Mary, my queen, my mother." He is buried in Holy Cross Cemetery on the campus of Stonehill College in North Easton, Massachusetts, among his fellow Holy Cross brothers.

The Church has thoroughly examined Fr. Peyton's life to see if he is worthy of being considered for sainthood. He has already passed two of four major steps, having received the titles Servant of God and Venerable. He will pass the third step of beatification if there is a miracle for which he is directly responsible. If we discover another miracle due to his intercession, he will qualify for canonization as a saint.

# THE JOYFUL MYSTERIES

The Joyful Mysteries are the first set of Rosary mysteries. They pulse with excitement and energy emanating from the Incarnation of the Son of God. These mysteries invite us to meditate on the early years of Jesus's life and the humble, obedient, and courageous faith of Mary, his mother.

The five Joyful Mysteries are the Annunciation, the Visitation, the Nativity, the Presentation in the Temple, and the Finding of the Child Jesus in the Temple.

The pilgrim's journey begins with the first Joyful Mystery, the Annunciation. The archangel Gabriel salutes Mary as full of grace and, responding to her perplexity, unfurls the majestic plan of God in her vocation to become the mother of the Savior. This event testifies to the power of faith and trust in God's plan, as Mary embraces her call from God to become the mother of the Redeemer.

The Visitation, the second Joyful Mystery, celebrates the meeting of Mary with her cousin Elizabeth, and the encounter of two children—John the Baptist and Jesus— in the wombs of their mothers. This mystery recognizes Mary as the first evangelist, the first person to bring the Word of God to another. Elizabeth's child leaps for joy at the arrival of Jesus in Mary's womb.

The Nativity is the third Joyful Mystery, commemorating the birth of Jesus in Bethlehem of Judea. This mystery celebrates the turning point in human history when God Incarnate sheds his light on a darkened world. No joy can equal the moment of bliss when a mother gazes for the first time upon her own child now come into the light of the world. Glory to God in the highest!

The Presentation, the fourth Joyful Mystery, recalls the moment when Mary and Joseph brought Jesus to the Temple in observance of the Jewish religious tradition of consecrating the firstborn male to God. The ecstasy of Simeon and Anna as they recognize Jesus as the savior of the world echoes the joy of grandparents everywhere in the birth of their children's children. The joy of this moment is tempered by Simeon's prophecy that this child will be a "sign that will be contradicted" and that "a sword will pierce" his mother's heart (Lk 2:34–35).

The Finding of the Child Jesus in the Temple is the fifth Joyful Mystery. This mystery introduces the drama of parents anxiously searching for a lost child, only to find him in the safety of a house of worship. There, Mary and Joseph discover the child listening and asking questions—"teaching" in his Father's house. This mystery reveals that even the most intimate human relationships take a back seat to the radical demands of the Gospel. As parents, relatives, and friends, we recall that we do not possess children or loved ones. They belong first to God, and we are to do all we can to honor this priority of grace.

# The Annunciation

## *Introduction*

Pray the Our Father.

## *Scripture Passage*

"In the sixth month, the angel Gabriel was sent from God to a town of Galilee called Nazareth, to a virgin betrothed to a man named Joseph, of the house of David, and the virgin's name was Mary" (Lk 1:26–27).

## *Reflection*

The turning point in human history took place in the small village of Nazareth more than two thousand years ago. Mary, a humble teenager, was at prayer when the archangel Gabriel greeted her as "full of grace" and disclosed a message of great importance. The eternal God had entrusted her with a unique vocation: to become the mother of God's Son, Jesus. Mary admitted she did not understand but, with confident faith and trust, readily embraced this stunning news as God's will for her.

Two years before his death, Fr. Patrick Peyton recalled the impact of his family's warm faith on his dawning love for Jesus and Mary. On the Feast of the Annunciation, March 25, 1990, from the Philippines, he wrote:

> In the morning of my life, God made the world around me and the people I lived with a mirror to reflect His Beauty, Goodness, and Love. . . . In my father's village, where I spent most of the nineteen years of my growing, I came very close to God. On Sundays, the roads like the spokes of a wheel reaching to its hub were dotted by small groupings of parishioners walking the winding roads to the chapel at the foothills of the mountains. In that chapel, the priest, the Mass, and the Tabernacle made Christ present. In my home, the Family Rosary prayed night after night, brought Mary to life. How true for me were the words of Shakespeare—"Tongues in trees, books in the running brooks, sermons in stone, and good in everything."[7]

Patrick's parents were so poor that the family often went to bed hungry, but they were rich in storing up for themselves "treasures in heaven, where neither moth nor decay destroys, nor thieves break in and steal" (Mt 6:20). These treasures, the fruit of a Rosary-praying family, set the heart of young Patrick on fire with love for God and his Blessed Mother, for the Church and the family. He knew that the family is God's masterpiece, our most precious possession. He grew up with the deep-seated conviction that the family is where life begins, faith is nurtured, hope matures, and love never ends. No wonder he proclaimed everywhere that "the family that prays together stays together."

Here with Mary at the Annunciation, we contemplate the mystery that God chose to come to us as a member of a human family.

## *Prayer*

Pray ten Hail Marys and one Glory Be.

## *Conclusion*

With Mary as a model for discernment, I place myself in your presence, Lord, and pray to grow in friendship with you. Let this day become a turning point in my life. Help me to turn more fully to you and your purpose for me. Give me the grace to know and embrace your will. Finally, Lord, with contrite heart, I ask you to forgive all the sins I am responsible for today. Good Lord, let your grace be upon me and my loved ones and all who are in any distress. Bless us all with your love and peace. Amen.

# The Visitation

## *Introduction*

Pray the Our Father.

## *Scripture Passage*

"During those days Mary set out and traveled to the hill country in haste to a town of Judah, where she entered the house of Zechariah and greeted Elizabeth. When Elizabeth heard Mary's greeting, the infant leaped in her womb, and Elizabeth, filled with the holy Spirit, cried out in a loud voice and said, 'Most blessed are you among women, and blessed is the fruit of your womb'" (Lk 1:39–42).

## *Reflection*

Mary is perhaps fifteen years old when she learns she is to be the Mother of God. The Holy Spirit conceives the child in her womb as soon as she utters a simple yes. But what happens after that yes? Does she remain home in Nazareth for fear of public shaming? Does she turn inward and seek to care only for the God in her womb? Does she keep this gift a secret from others?

Mary does none of these things. She allows God's self-gift to magnify her heart, her love, her world. She becomes the first evangelist, the first to bring the Word of God to others. As Fr. Peyton wrote, Mary knew that "to love God alone is not to love him at all." Jesus commanded us to love God *and* our neighbor. In doing so, Mary brings extraordinary joy to her cousin Elizabeth—and to all of us.

The Church exists to evangelize. Announcing and sharing the Good News of our salvation in Christ defines our mission. Like Mary, we are called to bring the Word to others.

## *Prayer*

Pray ten Hail Marys and one Glory Be.

## *Conclusion*

Lord, help me to share your life-giving Word at home and at work. Accept my grateful prayer for the example of Mary, the first evangelist. I also thank you, Lord, for family and friends who have shared their good news and love with me. I pray for peace in our world, in our homes, and in my heart. I thank you for the precious gift of another day. Amen.

# The Nativity

## *Introduction*

Pray the Our Father.

## *Scripture Passage*

"In those days a decree went out from Caesar Augustus that the whole world should be enrolled. This was the first enrollment, when Quirinius was governor of Syria. So all went to be enrolled, each to his own town. And Joseph too went up from Galilee from the town of Nazareth to Judea, to the city of David that is called Bethlehem, because he was of the house and family of David, to be enrolled with Mary, his betrothed, who was with child. While they were there, the time came for her to have her child, and she gave birth to her firstborn son. She wrapped him in swaddling clothes and laid him in a

manger, because there was no room for them in the inn"
(Lk 2:1–7).

## *Reflection*

Is there any scene more radiant and enchanting in all
human history than this Nativity tableau? Artists have
rendered it in paintings, sculptures, carvings, mosaics,
frescoes. Crèches around the world, from the Vatican
to the humblest outposts of humanity, celebrate it each
Christmas. They all include the child Jesus in the center; the Virgin Mother nearby; the serene foster father,
Joseph; the poor shepherds; the three mysterious wise
men from the East; and a bevy of farm animals.

The Nativity tells of the majestic and merciful movement of God to become human. His infinite love could
not be contained, so he joined our humanity. Jesus
became one with us so we can become one with God.
This realization fills us with hope, peace, and wondrous
joy.

This loving decision to share life with us moves us, in
turn, to reach out to neighbors, to people in need, and to
all those who are vulnerable and tired from their labors.
We keep them all in prayer and help them as we are able.

## *Prayer*

Pray ten Hail Marys and one Glory Be.

## *Conclusion*

Lord, grant me the grace of renewing my friendship with the Holy Family of Nazareth. Jesus, Mary, and Joseph model for us the magnetic attraction of unity, peace, and love found in the home. Deepen the harmony in our families. Thank you for the blessings of domestic life that give meaning, texture, and beauty to our lives. As always, Lord, keep us safe from the evil one. Amen.

# The Presentation
# in the Temple

## *Introduction*

Pray the Our Father.

## *Scripture Passage*

"When eight days were completed for his circumcision, he was named Jesus, the name given him by the angel before he was conceived in the womb. When the days were completed for their purification according to the law of Moses, they took him up to Jerusalem to present him to the Lord, just as it is written in the law of the Lord, 'Every male that opens the womb shall be consecrated to the Lord,' and to offer the sacrifice of 'a pair of turtledoves or two young pigeons,' in accordance with the dictate in the law of the Lord" (Lk 2:21–24).

## *Reflection*

Simeon and Anna embody the elderly grandparents of
every generation who are wise enough to have their pri-
orities in the right order. They know God comes first,
so they spend part of each day in the Temple, trusting
he will visit them. When he finally comes disguised as
an innocent babe in his mother's arms, Simeon rejoices
and prays,

> Now, Master, you may let your servant go
>     in peace, according to your word,
> for my eyes have seen your salvation,
>     which you prepared in sight of all the
>     peoples,
> a light for revelation to the Gentiles,
>     and glory for your people Israel. (Lk
>     2:29–32)

As a young Jewish lawyer, Raquel Zuckerman volun-
teered to assist Fr. Peyton in organizing a family Rosary
rally in downtown São Paulo, Brazil. Two million people attended the rally to hear his story. In later years, as
Raquel's father lay dying in the hospital, Fr. Peyton flew
from New York to be with the grieving family.

Raquel recalled that Fr. Peyton, upon arriving at
her father's hospital room, approached her mother and,
in a surprising gesture of respect, knelt before Mrs.

Zuckerman and asked for her blessing. Fr. Peyton said, "Any mother who could raise such a generous and faithful daughter must be very close to God. Please give me your blessing."

With this mystery of the Rosary, we thank God for our parents and grandparents. Many of them endured great hardships to provide for their children and to rear them as people of faith, integrity, and generosity.

### *Prayer*

Pray ten Hail Marys and one Glory Be.

### *Conclusion*

Lord, in our day, it is often the elders and grandparents who most lovingly share the faith with small children. Like Simeon and Anna, these elders in the faith are precious gifts to us. I thank you for them, Lord, and pray that young people will always value, respect, and listen to them. I ask you to forgive me for any unintentional neglect of the elders in my own family. Bless our grandparents with joy in knowing that we, like Joseph and Mary, love them and hold them in high esteem. Jesus, Mary, and Joseph, pray for us. Amen.

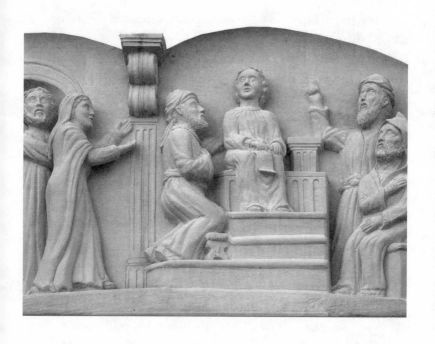

# The Finding of the Child Jesus in the Temple

*Introduction*

Pray the Our Father.

*Scripture Passage*

"Each year his parents went to Jerusalem for the feast of Passover, and when he was twelve years old, they went up according to festival custom. After they had completed its days, as they were returning, the boy Jesus remained behind in Jerusalem, but his parents did not know it. Thinking that he was in the caravan, they journeyed for a day and looked for him among their relatives and acquaintances, but not finding him, they returned to Jerusalem to look for him. After three days they found him in the temple, sitting in the midst of the teachers,

listening to them and asking them questions, and all who
heard him were astounded at his understanding and his
answers" (Lk 2:41–47).

## *Reflection*

Joseph and Mary faithfully kept all the religious rites of
observant Jews. Following the customs of their ancestors,
they journeyed to Jerusalem with the boy Jesus. After the
feasts, believing Jesus to be among the pilgrims returning to Nazareth, they became anxious when they could
not find him. After three days of frantic searching, Mary
and Joseph located him in the Temple conversing with
scholars of the Law.

Fr. Peyton himself experienced the great blessing of
a family rich in faith. He grew up in a Rosary-praying
home in Ireland where he came to know and love Mary,
the Mother of Jesus, Mother of the Church, his heavenly
mother and queen. The Hollywood actress Loretta Young
once said, "I never knew a man who loved a woman more
than Fr. Peyton loved the Blessed Mother."

The Holy Family of Nazareth reminds us that the
family is God's masterpiece. Fr. Peyton called the family
"our most precious possession"—the fundamental building block of society and Church. As goes the family, so
goes society.

## Prayer

Pray ten Hail Marys and one Glory Be.

## Conclusion

Lord, I thank you for my family—parents and grandparents, brothers and sisters, uncles and aunts, cousins and nieces and nephews. The family is where life begins, faith is nurtured, hope matures, and love never ends. I pray for our families to be healthy, happy, and holy. Forgive all our sins against you and each other. Grant us the grace to continue growing in wisdom and grace. Amen.

## *Week's End*

### *Saturday*

Pray all five Joyful Mysteries of the Rosary (see appendix B for guidance).

### *Sunday*

Here are the fruits of this week's prayer that I take with me to Sunday Mass:

_____

_____

_____

_____

_____

# THE LUMINOUS MYSTERIES

The Luminous Mysteries are the second set of Rosary mysteries. In 2002, St. John Paul II proposed this addition to the Rosary to complete the full cycle of the life of Christ from conception to full glorious revelation in heaven. These mysteries expand the pilgrim's journey through the Rosary to include the public ministry of Jesus, in which the light of Christ shines its warmth and brightness upon all creation.

The five Luminous Mysteries are the Baptism of Jesus, the Wedding at Cana, the Proclamation of the Kingdom, the Transfiguration, and the Institution of the Eucharist.

The first Luminous Mystery, the Baptism of Jesus, acts as a marker for the launch of Jesus's public ministry. In the drama of this mystery, Jesus, the Innocent One, descends into the waters bearing our sins upon his shoulders. He rises to the heavenly voice of the Father declaring him to be his beloved Son and the Holy Spirit anointing him for the mission he is to carry out. This mystery directly confirms that all who are baptized into Christ are anointed for a prophetic, priestly, and royal mission. Like the Master, we too are to announce the Good News to all.

The second Luminous Mystery is the Wedding at Cana, where Jesus performs the first of his signs. As described in John's gospel, Jesus turns water into wine at a wedding feast at the bidding of his mother, Mary. This action points to the desire of Jesus to sanctify the conjugal love of married couples and to recognize Mary as a principal intercessor in the community of believers. Jesus never says no to his mother. We too turn to Mary in our needs and follow her admonition to "do whatever he tells you" (Jn 2:5).

The Proclamation of the Kingdom, the third Luminous Mystery, centers our attention on the preaching of Jesus and the call to repentance, conversion, and reconciliation. Jesus forgives the sins of all who approach him in humble trust. He continues this ministry of divine mercy down through the ages in the Sacrament of Reconciliation, which he has entrusted to the Church. We personally benefit from the kingdom in our midst every time we confess our sins sincerely. Likewise, we must never tire of forgiving others and seeking their forgiveness when we have sinned against them and God.

The fourth Luminous Mystery, the Transfiguration, is the perfect Mystery of Light. In this mystery, the glory of God shines forth from the face of Christ and the voice of the Father commands Peter, James, and John to "listen to him" (Mk 9:7). This manifestation of God's presence and glory serves to strengthen the apostles for their suffering and confusion in the coming Passion and Death of Jesus. This vision of glory fortifies their faith so that they can follow Jesus to the joy of the Resurrection and take on lives transfigured by the Holy Spirit at Pentecost.

The Institution of the Eucharist, the fifth and final Luminous Mystery, draws us into the "source and summit of the Christian life" (*CCC* 1324), the Holy Sacrifice of the Mass. At the Last Supper, Jesus instituted the Sacrament of the Eucharist, commissioning the apostles to offer the new and eternal covenant in his Body and Blood for all nations and for all ages. This mystery places the Eucharist squarely in the center of our lives as Christians. It is in the Eucharist that the Lord speaks his word to our souls and nourishes us with the living Bread come down from heaven. Every time we celebrate the Eucharist with the priest and receive the Body and Blood of Christ, we are present with the Lord and the apostles at the Last Supper.

# The Baptism of Jesus

*Introduction*

Pray the Our Father.

*Scripture Passage*

"After Jesus was baptized, he came up from the water and behold, the heavens were opened [for him], and he saw the Spirit of God descending like a dove [and] coming upon him. And a voice came from the heavens, saying, 'This is my beloved Son, with whom I am well pleased'" (Mt 3:16–17).

*Reflection*

Jesus stood in line at the Jordan to be baptized by his cousin John. John's first encounter with Jesus was at the Visitation, when Mary traveled in haste to see Elizabeth, his mother. John receives Jesus as Elizabeth did, recognizing him as the salvation of the world. Jesus did not hold his status over his cousin—as St. Paul tells us, "Though he was in the form of God, [he] did not regard equality with God something to be grasped" (Phil 2:6).

When Jesus humbled himself to be baptized by John, he elevated that sacrament so that it could become for us a source of union with him. At St. Joseph Parish in the small village of Attymass, County Mayo, Ireland, Patrick Peyton was baptized into Christ in January 1909. On their wedding day, his parents, Mary and John Peyton, had promised each other and God to pray the Holy Rosary of the Blessed Virgin Mary every day in their home. Fulfilling this promise meant that young Patrick came to know and love Jesus and his mother Mary as true and real members of his family.

Throughout his life Fr. Peyton engaged in ongoing and lively dialogue with Mary. When diagnosed with terminal tuberculosis, he turned to Mary for help. His mentor, Fr. Cornelius Hagerty, CSC, announced to the dying Patrick that "Mary is alive!" and within months he experienced firsthand the proof of this statement in a gradual, gentle healing through Mary's intercession. He had no doubt that it was Mary who brought his case before the throne of God's mercy in answer to prayer. With equal certainty, he declared that Mary inspired him to commit his entire life as a priest to spreading the good news that "the family that prays together stays together." For him, family prayer achieved its loftiest height in the daily family Rosary.

## *Prayer*

Pray ten Hail Marys and one Glory Be.

## *Conclusion*

With gratitude to you, almighty God, I thank you for the gift of your beloved Son, Jesus, his mother Mary, and her son and disciple, Fr. Patrick Peyton. Forgive my distractions, timidity, lack of zeal, and failure to reflect your love today. Help me to realize that the mission given me by virtue of my baptism is a sharing in the mission of Christ and not my own will. Send your Spirit to set my soul on fire with love for you and my neighbor. Amen.

# The Wedding at Cana

## *Introduction*

Pray the Our Father.

## *Scripture Passage*

"On the third day there was a wedding in Cana in Galilee, and the mother of Jesus was there. Jesus and his disciples were also invited to the wedding. When the wine ran short, the mother of Jesus said to him, 'They have no wine.' [And] Jesus said to her, 'Woman, how does your concern affect me? My hour has not yet come.' His mother said to the servers, 'Do whatever he tells you'" (Jn 2:1–5).

## Reflection

On their wedding day, every couple exchanges the single life for married life, and as two become one, they give birth to a new family. Mary, the mother of Jesus, and the disciples were guests at a wedding at Cana in Galilee. The disciples witnessed the important role of Mary in bringing to the Lord's attention the need of the newly married couple to provide wine for their guests.

Without doubt, Mary brings our needs to God as well. Her famous last words in the gospel account of this event are memorable: "Do whatever he tells you." Following this instruction, Jesus proceeds to change ordinary water into a precious vintage (perhaps we can imagine a rich cabernet sauvignon). Soon he will go from changing water into wine to changing wine into his own blood at the Last Supper and at every Eucharist in every age and place.

The best advice Mary can give to married couples—to every person—is to "do whatever he tells you."

## Prayer

Pray ten Hail Marys and one Glory Be.

## *Conclusion*

Lord Jesus, when you performed the first miracle of your public ministry at Cana, you highlighted the sacramental nature of faithful, free, and fruitful love of husband and wife. In blessing married couples, you endow them with all the grace needed to become a true domestic Church. You give them the grace to love and honor each other as husband and wife in good times and in bad, in sickness and in health, for better or worse, until the end of earthly life. Help all married couples access these graces through regular family prayer and through service to each other. May their love be a sign to all of the fullness of your kingdom. Amen.

# The Proclamation of the Kingdom

## *Introduction*

Pray the Our Father.

## *Scripture Passage*

"Jesus came to Galilee proclaiming the gospel of God: 'This is the time of fulfillment. The kingdom of God is at hand. Repent, and believe in the gospel'" (Mk 1:14–15).

## *Reflection*

Fr. Peyton esteemed the family as the most effective bearer of the faith. As the conversations of the Second Vatican Council were articulated in its final documents, he championed the inclusion of the term "domestic

Church." He also welcomed the formal declaration of Mary as the Mother of the Church because she always leads her children to Our Lord for their salvation through the Catholic Church.

As members of God's royal family, we are called to speak God's saving words and share the richness of life in Christ with all we encounter. This is what Mary did as mother of our Savior, and we are called to follow the example of our mother in faith. The Lord promises to provide every spiritual blessing in the heavens so that we can share in this saving work. We access the grace for this mission through prayer, the sacraments, and trust in the Lord's promise to be with us always.

## Prayer

Pray ten Hail Marys and one Glory Be.

## Conclusion

Lord Jesus, I thank you for the blessings of this day and ask forgiveness for my sins against you and my neighbor. Help me to proclaim your kingdom in word and deed by following the example and inspiration of your mother. Like Mary, may I share your life with all those whom I meet. Grant me the grace to remain close to you in prayer, for you are the source of my strength. Amen.

# The Transfiguration

## *Introduction*

Pray the Our Father.

## *Scripture Passage*

"After six days Jesus took Peter, James, and John his brother, and led them up a high mountain by themselves. And he was transfigured before them; his face shone like the sun and his clothes became white as light" (Mt 17:1–2).

## *Reflection*

In psychology they call it a peak experience. Peter, James, and John were both frightened and awed by the sudden glory revealed in Christ, their friend and leader. Never in their wildest musings had they imagined such a spectacular manifestation of God's glory. Wow! Who is this Jesus whom Moses and Elijah treat with intimacy and deference? And that booming voice from out of the cloud still reverberating in their souls . . . what an incredible privilege to experience!

This moment is a gift from God to help Jesus's closest friends cope with the trials and tragedies that await them in the days to come.

## Prayer

Pray ten Hail Marys and one Glory Be.

## Conclusion

Almighty God, placing myself in your presence, I examine my conscience. I am tempted to focus on my little hurts, my impatience, my laziness. Help me also to remember the love, joy, and peace you radiate to us, despite our selfishness and self-preoccupation. Do not let me forget that your holy mountain is the highest of all mountains and that it is here, with your Son, that we are set on fire again with the wonder, warmth, and wisdom of the Spirit. Please give me the grace to deal with my shortcomings and renew my love for you and others. Amen.

*Friday*

# The Institution
# of the Eucharist

*Introduction*

Pray the Our Father.

*Scripture Passage*

"While they were eating, Jesus took bread, said the blessing, broke it, and giving it to his disciples said, 'Take and eat; this is my body'" (Mt 26:26).

*Reflection*

Fr. Peyton's maternal grandfather, Robert Gillard, was confined to the house due to age and illness. When Patrick was eight, he stayed home with his grandfather while the rest of the family went to Mass. His grandfather's devotion during this time so impressed Patrick that he wrote the following, years later:

> On Sunday mornings Grandfather dressed up with the greatest care. He had a white shirt with a starched front and winged collar, new trousers and new bedroom slippers. He was shaved and spic and span and he would say, when it came time for Mass, "What time is it. Now tell me just when it's eleven o'clock." Then he knelt and devoutly said his Rosary . . . the fifteen decades . . . and at the end of his Rosary he would say, "Do you think Mass is over now?" When we assured him that it was, he would bless himself devoutly and then sat and waited for his family to return from Mass.[8]

The Eucharist unites us to Christ and each other, sustaining us spiritually with food for the journey of life. Fr. Peyton reverently celebrated the Eucharist every day of his life as a priest. He entrusted to the Eucharistic Lord all his major decisions by physically placing letters and petitions before the Lord reserved in the tabernacle.

## Prayer

Pray ten Hail Marys and one Glory Be.

## *Conclusion*

Lord Jesus, during the Last Supper, you washed the feet of your disciples, teaching us that only you can cleanse us of all stains of sin. Help me remember that to prepare well for Eucharistic communion, I must turn to you for forgiveness. Then, with a pure heart, may I receive all the graces you wish to give me in Holy Communion. Bread of Life, I ask your blessing upon my family and friends. Thank you for sharing your abiding presence—your very Body and Blood—with us in the Eucharist. Amen.

## *Week's End*

### *Saturday*

Pray all five Luminous Mysteries of the Rosary (see appendix B for guidance).

### *Sunday*

Here are the fruits of this week's prayer that I take with me to Sunday Mass:

_____

_____

_____

_____

_____

# THE SORROWFUL MYSTERIES

The third set of Rosary mysteries, the Sorrowful Mysteries, guide the pilgrim through the events that mark the suffering and death of Jesus. These mysteries not only tell us of the price Jesus paid for our justification, redemption, and salvation but also help us appreciate his profound love for us.

The five Sorrowful Mysteries are the Agony in the Garden, the Scourging at the Pillar, the Crowning with Thorns, the Carrying of the Cross, and the Crucifixion.

The Agony in the Garden begins the Sorrowful Mysteries. In Gethsemane, Jesus encounters anguish in the hours leading to his arrest, torture, humiliation, and suffering on the Cross. With the weight of all the sins of humanity bearing down upon him, he says yes to the Father and reverses the no of Adam and Eve in the Garden of Paradise. We too must face moments of anguish in saying yes to God and no to sin and darkness.

The Scourging at the Pillar, the second Sorrowful Mystery, tells of the brutality of Roman torture and punishment. Jesus's love for each of us impelled him to endure this harsh treatment so that we might know that our own suffering can have purpose and meaning when united to his.

The third Sorrowful Mystery, the Crowning with Thorns, details the mocking and degradation of the innocent Savior. He becomes a plaything for the cruel occupiers of the Jewish people. Like Jesus, many today suffer from poverty, misunderstanding, loneliness, and a lack of love. May the Lord open our eyes to his presence among those in our midst who are most in need of our love and attention.

The Carrying of the Cross, the fourth Sorrowful Mystery, reminds us of our dependence on others for help in bearing our burdens. As Jesus needs the assistance of Simon of Cyrene, so we must acknowledge our limitations and humbly ask for and accept help from others when we are in genuine need. When we do so, we give others the opportunity to serve Christ and come to know him better.

The Crucifixion, the fifth and final Sorrowful Mystery, delivers the great paradox: it is the saddest yet most hopeful event in human history. How can this be? It is sad because the Lord of life and love truly died for us on the Cross. Yet it is also hopeful because this sacrifice transformed the Cross into our means of salvation.

# The Agony in the Garden

## *Introduction*

Pray the Our Father.

## *Scripture Passage*

"Then Jesus came with them to a place called Gethsemane, and he said to his disciples, 'Sit here while I go over there and pray.' He took along Peter and the two sons of Zebedee, and began to feel sorrow and distress. Then he said to them, 'My soul is sorrowful even to death. Remain here and keep watch with me.' He advanced a little and fell prostrate in prayer, saying, 'My Father, if it is possible, let this cup pass from me; yet, not as I will, but as you will'" (Mt 26:36–39).

## *Reflection*

Patrick Peyton knew the suffering of poverty in his childhood in Ireland. He also knew the suffering of rejection when he longed to serve as a missionary but was dismissed by various religious orders. His most prolonged suffering was a yearlong bout with tuberculosis that was gradually wasting his body and his confidence in God.

Believing he was dying, Fr. Peyton faced the choice of giving up completely or surrendering to God and asking the Mother of God for help. After a protracted struggle in mind and spirit as well as in body, he chose life. The sacrifices offered by his mother and his sister, as well as the prayers of other family members, Holy Cross brothers, and many friends strengthened him during this time.

Jesus was alone during his agony in the Garden of Gethsemane, so his Father sent an angel to strengthen him (Lk 22:43). With God on our side, we are never alone.

## *Prayer*

Pray ten Hail Marys and one Glory Be.

## *Conclusion*

Eternal Father, open my mind and heart to praise you for all the blessings you shower upon me. Give me the grace to desire your will, to know it, to embrace it, and to accomplish it fully, quickly, and gladly. Send your angels to strengthen my prayer and deepen my faith. Help me to trust you, especially when I am facing darkness and uncertainty. Amen.

# The Scourging at the Pillar

## *Introduction*

Pray the Our Father.

## *Scripture Passage*

"Then he released Barabbas to them, but after he had Jesus scourged, he handed him over to be crucified" (Mt 27:26).

## *Reflection*

Our world is scourged by global pandemics, by wars, by natural disasters, by famine. These all lead to loss of control at work, at home, at school, in religious devotions, and in our socializing and leisure. Perhaps they lead to loss of control of health and ultimately life itself. What are we to do?

"God whispers to us in our pleasures, speaks to us in our conscience, but shouts in our pains; it is his megaphone to rouse a deaf world." The holy preacher Venerable Fulton Sheen loved this C. S. Lewis quote and repeated it often. He said, "I feel so sad when I walk past most hospitals because I know there is so much pain, but it is wasted, when it could be such a blessing for others if it were united to the sufferings of Christ."

In his Passion, Jesus lost control over his own body. At the Last Supper, he turned wine into blood, and a day later, his blood was poured out like wine as a libation for our redemption. No one welcomes pain, but to accept it as Jesus and the saints do is to sanctify it and render it life-giving for ourselves, our neighbors, and the world.

## Prayer

Pray ten Hail Marys and one Glory Be.

## Conclusion

Lord Jesus, I do not need a cat-o'-nine-tails to scourge others. With my words I wound others by gossiping, attributing false motives, giving unfair criticism, not listening with my full attention. Help me to be more aware of how my selfishness damages the dignity of others. With a sorrowful heart, I turn to you for forgiveness. Give me strength to love as you did. Amen.

# The Crowning with Thorns

## *Introduction*

Pray the Our Father.

## *Scripture Passage*

"Then the soldiers of the governor took Jesus inside the praetorium and gathered the whole cohort around him. They stripped off his clothes and threw a scarlet military cloak about him. Weaving a crown out of thorns, they placed it on his head, and a reed in his right hand. And kneeling before him, they mocked him, saying, 'Hail, King of the Jews!'" (Mt 27:27–29).

## *Reflection*

There is so much suffering around us. The elderly and infirm, for example, experience loneliness and the pain of age-related illnesses. Although they do not wear a literal crown of thorns, they clearly participate in the sufferings of Christ.

Think, too, of the healthcare professionals who tend to the sick and infirm in nursing homes, hospitals, and private homes. At times they place their own health at risk as they strive to minister to those in their care. During times of pandemic, severe weather, natural disasters, and war, these angels of mercy keep coming to their labors and, like good shepherds, care for the flock entrusted to them. Exhaustion and anxiety do not prevent the best caregivers from seeing the sufferings of their patients as a participation in the suffering of Christ crowned with thorns.

In whatever sufferings we face, we can turn to Christ, who suffered with and for us. Uniting ourselves with him in our pain and loss of control is another way to grow in intimacy with him, to rest in his love for us, and to trust him to bring us to new life.

## Prayer

Pray ten Hail Marys and one Glory Be.

## Conclusion

Almighty God, I thank you for never abandoning me to my suffering and sinfulness. By trusting in your grace and Mary's maternal support, I can overcome disappointment and apparent defeat. I ask your mercy and forgiveness for sometimes doubting your providential care for me and my family. Help me to rely on your love when I need it most. Amen.

# The Carrying of the Cross

## *Introduction*
Pray the Our Father.

## *Scripture Passage*
"They pressed into service a passer-by, Simon, a Cyrenian, who was coming in from the country, the father of Alexander and Rufus, to carry his cross. They brought him to the place of Golgotha (which is translated Place of the Skull)" (Mk 15:21–22).

## *Reflection*
The wounded, humiliated, and dying Christ staggers and falls beneath the weight of the Cross. Though his blood purples the hard, stony earth, he refuses to give up.

Despite the staggering evil arrayed against him, he rises again and again, making his way to Calvary.

The figures who are unafraid to accompany him through his suffering, death, and burial are mostly women. Veronica wipes his brow with her veil; brave women of Jerusalem "mourned and lamented him" (Lk 23:27) on his way; two women join Mary his mother at the foot of the Cross (Jn 19:25). These women display the capacity to bear great suffering with faithfulness.

As a seminarian preparing for the priesthood, Patrick Peyton endured a heavy cross of bodily and spiritual suffering when he contracted tuberculosis. Only after he surrendered to God's will and begged for healing through the intercession of the Mother of Sorrows did he become a man of hope.

Two heroic women—his mother, Mary Peyton; and his sister, Nellie Peyton—made his cross of suffering bearable. Both asked God to give them Patrick's suffering and to take their lives in return for allowing him to be a good and holy priest. After his mother's death, Patrick received a letter from his aunt that said, "Your mother got her wish. Her constant prayer was that all your sufferings would come upon her and that you would get well and go back to your work."

After his sister Nellie's death, Patrick was given a note that she left in her room: "I, Nellie Peyton, offer Thee, dear Lord, all my thoughts, words, and actions of this day, and every day, and even life itself, for my two brothers, Thomas Francis Peyton and Patrick Joseph Peyton, that if it be Thy Holy Will that they become priests, that never in their priestly lives will they commit a mortal sin."

Lord, bless all the women who bear the burden of caring for others during sobering and trying days.

## Prayer

Pray ten Hail Marys and one Glory Be.

## Conclusion

Jesus our Savior, I ask forgiveness for the times I avoid the crosses you send me. In my eager pursuit of comfort, I turn down opportunities to grow in your grace by shouldering these crosses, both large and small. As I recall those at home, work, church, and in social services who willingly take up their cross each day in order to make life bearable and even a joy for others, I give you thanks. Fill us with deep gratitude for them and for your suffering on the way of the Cross for our salvation. Amen.

*Friday*

# The Crucifixion

*Introduction*

Pray the Our Father.

*Scripture Passage*

"When they came to the place called the Skull, they crucified him and the criminals there, one on his right, the other on his left. [Then Jesus said, 'Father, forgive them, they know not what they do.'] They divided his garments by casting lots. The people stood by and watched; the rulers, meanwhile, sneered at him and said, 'He saved others, let him save himself if he is the chosen one, the Messiah of God.' Even the soldiers jeered at him. As they approached to offer him wine they called out, 'If you are King of the Jews, save yourself.' Above him there was an inscription that read, 'This is the King of the Jews.'

Now one of the criminals hanging there reviled Jesus, saying, 'Are you not the Messiah? Save yourself and us.' The other, however, rebuking him, said in reply, 'Have you no fear of God, for you are subject to the same condemnation? And indeed, we have been condemned justly, for the sentence we received corresponds to our crimes, but this man has done nothing criminal.' Then he said, 'Jesus, remember me when you come into your kingdom.' He replied to him, 'Amen, I say to you, today you will be with me in Paradise.'

"It was now about noon and darkness came over the whole land until three in the afternoon because of an eclipse of the sun. Then the veil of the temple was torn down the middle. Jesus cried out in a loud voice, 'Father, into your hands I commend my spirit'; and when he had said this he breathed his last" (Lk 23:33–46).

## *Reflection*

By his Passion and Death, the Son of God demonstrates how perfect and total his love is. Even as he languishes upon the Cross, he continues giving to the very end: forgiveness for our sins, heaven for the repentant thief, hope for eternal life to believers. Finally, and best of all, he gives his mother to the Beloved Disciple and to us, and his spirit to his heavenly Father.

The price Christ paid is captured in Michelangelo's *Pieta*, that most beautiful work of art that also shows the world the profound wound suffered by the Mother of Sorrows. Patrick Peyton loved the *Pieta* and lingered before this precious sculpture for hours on end in St. Peter's Basilica at the Vatican.

As she cradles her dead son in her arms, places him in the tomb, and departs, Mary truly is Our Lady of Sorrows and Mother of Hope. Whenever Fr. Peyton's friends looked for him at the Vatican, they knew where they were likely to find him—at the basilica's entrance, praying the Rosary before the *Pieta*.

## Prayer

Pray ten Hail Marys and one Glory Be.

## Conclusion

Lord Jesus Christ, as I place myself in your presence, help me to listen with the ear of the heart and to see with the eyes of faith the grand and moving events of your Passion and Death. May the knowledge of your love poured out for us on the Cross spur me on to share your Good News with all I meet. Be near to all who are in need. Help us to know that our only true hope for healing is through your Cross. Amen.

## *Week's End*

### *Saturday*

Pray all five Sorrowful Mysteries of the Rosary (see appendix B for guidance).

### *Sunday*

Here are the fruits of this week's prayer that I take with me to Sunday Mass:

_____

_____

_____

_____

_____

# THE GLORIOUS MYSTERIES

The fourth set of Rosary mysteries, the Glorious Mysteries, uplift us with the hope-filled events of the Resurrection and what followed. These mysteries draw the pilgrim into the climactic events of salvation history as Jesus opens to us the bright promise of eternal life.

The five Glorious Mysteries are the Resurrection, the Ascension, the Descent of the Holy Spirit, the Assumption, and the Coronation of Mary.

While we look to the Cross of Jesus with hope, our faith is centered on the Resurrection. This first Glorious Mystery celebrates that Jesus rose from the dead on the third day after his Crucifixion. Just as we have been baptized into Christ's death, so may we rise to new life with him on the last day. All who die in God's friendship have this promise of eternal life. Nothing is more beautiful than to speak of our friendship with Christ and to share it with all we meet.

The second Glorious Mystery, the Ascension, is recorded in the Acts of the Apostles. In this mystery, the apostles witness Jesus rising to heaven to be seated at the right hand of the Father to intercede for us always. Through our baptism, we too, in a mystical way, are already seated with Jesus at the Father's right hand in heaven. Even now we can bask in the love and beauty of the heavenly realm with Jesus, Mary, the angels, and all the saints.

The third Glorious Mystery is the Descent of the Holy Spirit. In this mystery, while Mary and the apostles are at prayer, the Holy Spirit descends upon them in the form of tongues of fire. He emboldens the apostles and sends them out to proclaim the Good News to all the world. As a different sort of spiritual exercise, try using your rosary beads to pray to the Holy Spirit. As you move through the beads with your fingers, pray the beautiful words "Come, Holy Spirit" on each of the beads. This simple prayer invites the greatest goodness in heaven and on earth to strengthen you with the joy of the Gospel.

The fourth Glorious Mystery celebrates the Assumption of Mary into heaven, body and soul, at the end of her earthly life. This event is something we perceive with the eyes of faith. Where Mary has gone, we hope to follow.

She is the mother of all believers, entrusted to us by her son on the Cross. She is the Mother of the Church. She is the Mother of Mercy. Let us honor her and follow her, for she loves nothing more than to bring us to her son, Jesus.

The fifth Glorious Mystery, the Coronation of Mary, is the capstone of the mysteries of the Rosary. The Coronation raises us to the heavenly realms of angels and saints. In this mystical world, we honor Mary not only as mother but as Queen of Heaven and Earth. Still a creature, she is the proudest boast of the human race. It was her yes to God in the beginning that set in motion the great pilgrim journey of the People of God to make God known, loved, and served.

# The Resurrection

## *Introduction*

Pray the Our Father.

## *Scripture Passage*

"But at daybreak on the first day of the week they took the spices they had prepared and went to the tomb. They found the stone rolled away from the tomb; but when they entered, they did not find the body of the Lord Jesus. While they were puzzling over this, behold, two men in dazzling garments appeared to them. They were terrified and bowed their faces to the ground. They said to them, 'Why do you seek the living one among the dead? He is not here, but he has been raised'" (Lk 24:1–6).

## *Reflection*

The women who discover an open, empty tomb on Easter morning are filled with wonder and confusion. Their amazement only increases when heavenly visitors tell them that Jesus has risen from the dead. They arrived at the tomb prepared for a sorrowful conclusion to their experience of Jesus by anointing his body. Instead, they discovered a new beginning!

In a Regina Caeli address in 1996, St. John Paul II referred to the Resurrection as "the strength, the secret of Christianity." This historical event, attested to by the women at the tomb and many others whom Jesus appeared to later, is the foundation of our faith and the Church—it is our source of hope. St. John Paul II encourages us to relive this moment with Mary. "Even in the darkness of Good Friday she prepared herself to receive the light of Easter morning," he said. "Let us ask her to obtain for us a deep faith in this extraordinary event, which is salvation and hope for the world."[9]

It is difficult to number the lasting contributions St. John Paul II made to the Church in his twenty-six-plus years as pope. Through it all, he maintained the confident assertion that the power of the Death and Resurrection of Jesus Christ is greater than all the forces of evil. Be not afraid to open the door to Christ, the risen Lord. He has conquered sin and death. Alleluia!

## Prayer

Pray ten Hail Marys and one Glory Be.

## Conclusion

Almighty God, I thank you for the gift of our Catholic faith, which teaches us that the risen Jesus lives in so many places—in Mary, in our church tabernacles, in the poor, in our hearts. Help me to align the internal and external elements of my faith so that I will give witness to you in my thoughts, words, and deeds. Accept my gratitude for your goodness and help me to remember my brothers and sisters in need. Amen.

# The Ascension

*Introduction*

Pray the Our Father.

*Scripture Passage*

"So then the Lord Jesus, after he spoke to them, was taken up into heaven and took his seat at the right hand of God" (Mk 16:19).

*Reflection*

After the Resurrection, the apostles and Mary experienced an in-between time. They knew the Lord had risen from the dead but had not yet been given the Holy Spirit to share this Good News. After Jesus ascended into heaven, they gathered each day in prayer with Mary and some of the other women to prepare for what came next.

Mary was the glue that held them together, constantly reminding them of Jesus by her quiet presence.

Daily prayer with Mary played a decisive role in the life of the young Patrick Peyton as he was dying from tuberculosis. After he was healed through Mary's intercession, he searched for a suitable way to express his gratitude to God and the Blessed Mother. Two years later, after he was ordained a priest, he found the answer to his search: he would encourage millions to also join Mary in daily prayer.

Fr. Peyton set out to start a family Rosary movement—to gather millions of American families to pledge to pray the Rosary daily. With the fervor and zeal of the apostles, he began a campaign that reached tens of millions around the globe, far exceeding his initial goal. Until his last breath, he did not cease praying for families and reminding them that "the family that prays together stays together."

## Prayer

Pray ten Hail Marys and one Glory Be.

## Conclusion

Lord, as I place myself in your presence, help me to know that Mary is always with me, as she was with the apostles in the Upper Room, supporting me with her prayers. I thank you for your abundant blessings. Open the minds and hearts of all to the great power of regular family prayer. With your mother's help, may I share your Good News by the witness of my life, that others may come to know your saving love. Amen.

# The Descent of the Holy Spirit

*Introduction*

Pray the Our Father.

*Scripture Passage*

"When the time for Pentecost was fulfilled, they were all in one place together. And suddenly there came from the sky a noise like a strong driving wind, and it filled the entire house in which they were. Then there appeared to them tongues as of fire, which parted and came to rest on each one of them. And they were all filled with the holy Spirit and began to speak in different tongues, as the Spirit enabled them to proclaim" (Acts 2:1–4).

## *Reflection*

After the Holy Spirit descended upon the disciples, they were strengthened and emboldened to go out across the world to preach the Gospel. They were unable to contain the Good News—they had to go out and share it, even to the point of martyrdom. And people were moved by their witness; thousands converted and joined their faith in the risen Lord.

In Golden Gate Park in San Francisco on October 7, 1961, more than half a million people assembled to pray, adore the Lord, and listen to the testimony of Fr. Peyton. This Rosary rally remains the largest religious gathering in American history, surpassing even St. John Paul II's World Youth Day event in Denver, Colorado, in 1993. With more than forty such mass Rosary rallies from 1948 to 1987, Patrick Peyton spoke live and in person to more than twenty-eight million people.

Armies of volunteers and leaders from all sectors collaborated to organize these rallies, but they would never have gathered so many people without the help of the Holy Spirit. Fr. Peyton made sure preparations included weeks of organized prayer and preaching. Organizers promised to fast and offer their suffering for the success of the rally. These actions invited the Holy Spirit as the driving force behind the rallies, and the crowds responded to that energy and witness. They could see that something special was happening and wanted to be part of it.

That's the power of the Spirit in our lives: it brings the Gospel to life in us so that it spills over into the rest of the world.

## Prayer

Pray ten Hail Marys and one Glory Be.

## Conclusion

God of life, I ask you to send your Spirit to me as you sent the Spirit to the disciples. Renew my faith and purpose by helping me to place you above all else. Give me wisdom, understanding, counsel, fortitude, knowledge, piety, and a sense of awe and wonder at your presence. Deepen my faith that I may reveal your love through my life, for the world needs this Good News. Amen.

# The Assumption

*Introduction*

Pray the Our Father.

*Scripture Passage*

"Behold, from now on will all ages call me blessed. The Mighty One has done great things for me, and holy is his name" (Lk 1:48–49).

*Reflection*

At the Ascension, Jesus rose to heaven—body and soul, humanity and divinity—where he is now seated at the right hand of the Father. No wonder, then, that he would desire to have his mother with him to enjoy for all eternity the bliss of heaven with the Father and the Holy Spirit and all the angels and saints. Mary is fully human, and her assumption into heaven, body and soul, indicates to us that where she has gone, we can hope to follow. In the meantime, we have a powerful advocate in Mary at the throne of grace.

No country was dearer to Fr. Peyton's Family Rosary Crusade than the Philippines. The initial Rosary rally in Manila in 1959 drew a gathering of 1.5 million people in Luneta Park to pray the Rosary and listen to Fr. Peyton's moving testimony. In 1962, two million people came to the Rosary rally in Cebu, the birthplace of Christianity in the Philippines.

Cardinal Jaime Sin, the late archbishop of Manila, attributed the peaceful overthrow of the Philippine dictatorship in 1986 to the special intervention of the Blessed Mother at what is now called the Miracle at EDSA. It began in 1985, when more than two million people attended a Rosary rally at Luneta Park. The following year, when the regime rigged the presidential election of 1986, several million people protested peacefully against the outrage. Families, nuns, and leaders of the people faced down the military with Rosaries and roses. Cardinal Sin said many of those who attended reported seeing the Blessed Mother in the heavens above the rally.

Prayer has the power to change a society from dictatorship to democracy. Let us approach Mary, knowing that she cares for us and will bring us to her son.

## *Prayer*

Pray ten Hail Marys and one Glory Be.

## *Conclusion*

Lord, the example of Mary our mother fills me with hope. She was close to you during her life on earth, and as our mother in faith, she invites us into this closeness as well. Mary now watches over us from her place at your right hand in heaven and intercedes powerfully for her children in distress. I pray she will bring me home to you at the conclusion of my life. Amen.

# The Coronation of Mary

## *Introduction*

Pray the Our Father.

## *Scripture Passage*

"A great sign appeared in the sky, a woman clothed with the sun, with the moon under her feet, and on her head a crown of twelve stars" (Rv 12:1).

## *Reflection*

On Mother's Day, May 13, 1945, Fr. Patrick Peyton planned to broadcast a National Day of Prayer for peace in Europe. He had cajoled the leadership of the second-largest radio network in America, the Mutual Broadcasting System, to give him gratis a half-hour time slot on Sunday morning. But just the week prior,

President Harry Truman suddenly announced peace in Europe, so Fr. Peyton altered his focus to a prayer of thanksgiving to God.

Fr. Peyton approached Elsie Dick, director of religious programming for the New York broadcasting company. His plan included a national half-hour radio spot with the Rosary led by the Sullivan family of Waterloo, Iowa. Five brothers in this family had died when their ship, the USS *Juneau*, sank in the Pacific theater.

Elsie rejected the proposal, which propelled the young Irish immigrant priest into anguish. He began desperately fighting for his plan. Before a pivotal meeting with her, he prayed his favorite appeal to the Blessed Mother, the Memorare. After challenging Elsie to do more than spout words to support the family, she relented.

The program featured a welcome by Archbishop Francis Spellman of New York, who called thirty-six-year-old Fr. Patrick Peyton the "American apostle of the family Rosary." The Sullivans prayed the Glorious Mysteries, and Bing Crosby, who was at the height of his popularity, delivered a passionate plea for the family Rosary. The program concluded with a recorded message from President Truman declaring a National Day of Thanksgiving followed by a brief message from Fr. Peyton, who dedicated the program to the world's greatest mother, Mary.

Fr. Peyton begged listeners to become lifelong apostles of the family Rosary, saying, "And on this day promise Mary that you will do all in your power to change the homes of the world into homes where God and Mary will be forever honored by the daily Family Rosary."

It was a smashing national success, and Fr. Peyton attributed it all to Mary's intercession. The popularity of the event prompted Fr. Peyton to move to Hollywood and take advantage of radio—and eventually television and film—alongside Hollywood celebrities to advance his mission to encourage families to pray the Rosary.

## Prayer

Pray ten Hail Marys and one Glory Be.

## Conclusion

Lord, Fr. Peyton's final words before he died were barely audible—he simply whispered, "Mary, my queen, my mother." Thank you for the witness and example of Fr. Peyton. May I embrace Mary as my queen just as he did, for she always leads us to her son, Jesus. Through the intercession of Mary, Queen of Heaven, may we grow in faith, hope, and love and bring your peace to the world. Amen.

## *Week's End*

### *Saturday*

Pray all five Glorious Mysteries of the Rosary (see appendix B for guidance).

### *Sunday*

Here are the fruits of this week's prayer that I take with me to Sunday Mass:

_____

_____

_____

_____

_____

APPENDIX A:

# The History of the Rosary

Like the air we breathe or God's grace, the Rosary is everywhere! You don't need to look far to glimpse rosary beads ornamenting the necks of such celebrities as Lady Gaga or Mark Wahlberg, or dangling from the rearview mirrors of countless cars, buses, and trucks. Beyond ornamentation, these blessed beads help millions to pray every moment of every day. Rosary devotees are of all ages, races, ethnicities, cultures, social classes, and lifestyles. Except for the Holy Eucharist, there isn't a more popular or iconic instrument of prayer than the Rosary anywhere on God's earth. Where did the Rosary come from, and why is it so popular?

The Rosary has existed for at least eight hundred years, and perhaps much longer, as an important devotion in Catholic life. Tracing the Rosary's history means embarking on a surprising adventure replete with unexpected twists, turns, and miracles.

The Rosary's ancient roots stretch far back into the early history of Judaism and Christianity with two practices: praying all of the one hundred and fifty psalms in the Old Testament, and the near-universal religious practice of keeping track of prayers by counting with beads, pebbles, or marks on wood or stone.

The psalms emerged from early Hebrew oral traditions and later writings attributed to King David, King Solomon, and various court scribes and poets. In Jesus's day, pious observant Jews prayed the psalms especially in the liturgy and in private devotions. The gospels testify that Jesus himself prayed the psalms often. This practice continued into the early Christian centuries. Monks and nuns fled to the desert and its tranquility to grow in silent friendship with God. Soon they were praying together in community with psalms copied manually on papyrus or lambskin scrolls.

Most people did not have access to psalm scrolls (nor could they read or understand Latin, Greek, or Hebrew/Aramaic), but they still wished to share the beautiful, inspiring prayer life of the early church. Rather than memorize all one hundred and fifty psalms, they began substituting other more common prayers for the psalms, such as the Our Father. They grouped the prayers into sets of fifty and counted small pebbles to keep track of how many they had prayed.

The earliest accounts of the Rosary as we know it today arise around the time of St. Dominic (1170–1221), founder of the Order of Preachers (known as the Dominicans). Called by many the "Father of the Rosary," he was central to its origin and promotion. He was the first to encourage the widespread teaching of this sacred devotion.

Dominican friars and many popes share an account of a mystical experience in which St. Dominic received a rosary from the very hands of the Virgin Mary in the year 1208. While the authenticity of this account is not certain, Dominic's role as a foundational promoter of the devotion is.

Rosary prayer continued growing and evolving through the centuries. Following a historic event in 1571, the highest authority in the Catholic Church granted official recognition of the Rosary for all believers. In that year, Pope St. Pius V asked all Christians to pray the Rosary for help in defending Christian Europe from the invading Ottoman Turks. At a major engagement at sea on October 7, 1571, the Battle of Lepanto, the Christian armada unexpectedly and spectacularly triumphed over the much larger Ottoman fleet. With this victory, the Christian people recognized the power of the Rosary.

Since then, Catholics have celebrated the Feast of the Holy Rosary on October 7.

Many popes and saints have endorsed the Rosary as a magnificent means of growing spiritually. St. Louis de Montfort (1673–1716) created the Confraternity of the Rosary, a religious association dedicated to the devotion. Pope Leo XIII (1810–1903) was the greatest champion of the Rosary ever to sit in the Chair of Peter. He wrote eleven encyclicals on the Rosary, promulgated numerous apostolic letters on the devotion, and delivered countless messages on the Rosary to various dioceses and religious institutes.

Above all this history, Venerable Patrick Peyton, CSC (1909–1992), is preeminent among modern advocates of the Rosary as a devotion that can save the family, the Church, and society. In 1942 he founded the Family Rosary Crusade, which reached around the globe to proclaim that "the family that prays together stays together." More than twenty-eight million people attended his Rosary rallies, supporting his belief that "a world at prayer is a world at peace."

Finally, we have to acknowledge the role of the great theologian and philosopher St. John Paul II (1920–2005), who proclaimed in his first week in the Chair of Peter that "the Rosary is my favorite prayer." His apostolic exhortation *Rosarium Virginis Mariae* raised up the Rosary for all to ponder anew as a tremendous instrument of grace and endowed the devotion with fresh theological and spiritual heft. St. John Paul II, reformed the Rosary for the first time in nearly five hundred years by adding the five Luminous Mysteries, focused on the public ministry of the Lord Jesus.

St. John Paul II articulated the spiritual benefits of praying the Rosary:

- The Rosary is a memorial by which Mary constantly sets before us the mysteries of her son;

- The Rosary is an invaluable source of self-discovery and integration;

- The Rosary is a sublime encounter of divine friendship;

- The Rosary unites us to the bond between Jesus and Mary;

- The Rosary is a supreme source of comfort and solace;

- The Rosary is a condensed version of the gospels.

He explained that the Rosary is a "simple yet profound" way for people of all ages to explore and experience milestone events in the life of Christ, guided by the pure love and sure confidence of Mary, our mother.

To these benefits, we can add two more dimensions. First, as Romano Guardini says, "To pray the Rosary is to linger in the domain of Mary." Mary is truly our mother, and she blesses us with her maternal love and joy every time we invoke her assistance in the Rosary. Second, praying the Rosary before celebrating the Eucharist is an excellent way to focus on Our Lord and his Mystical Body, the Church. The Rosary helps to clear away distractions and opens our hearts to the Holy Spirit's fire and love in the Mass.

> O Jesus, living in Mary,
> Come and live in your servants,
> In the spirit of holiness,
> In the fullness of your power,
> In the perfection of your ways,
> In the truth of your virtues,
> In the communion of your mysteries.
> Rule over every adverse power, in your
>     Spirit,
> for the glory of the Father.
> Amen.
> —Jean-Jacques Olier, SS (1608–1657)

# How to Pray the Rosary

To pray the Rosary, we recite a series of prayers while reflecting on events from the life of Christ—his Incarnation and hidden years in Jerusalem (Joyful Mysteries), his proclamation of God's kingdom (Luminous Mysteries), his Passion and Death (Sorrowful Mysteries), and his Resurrection and Ascension (Glorious Mysteries). The final two sets of Glorious Mysteries are meditations on Mary's assumption into heaven and her coronation as Queen of Heaven and Earth.

The recitation of prayers is not the focus of praying the Rosary. Rather, their repetitive nature serves as a type of mantra in a regular rhythm that keeps us centered on the particular mystery on which we are meditating. Praying the Rosary is divided into three parts: the opening, the body, and the conclusion.

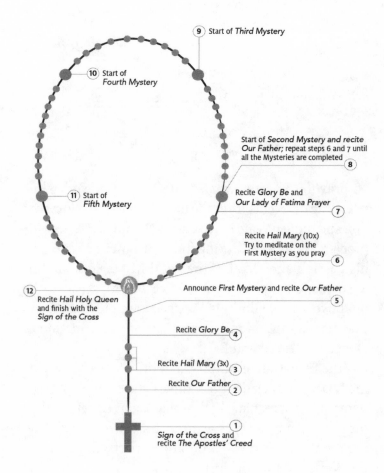

**9** Start of *Third Mystery*

**10** Start of *Fourth Mystery*

Start of *Second Mystery* and recite *Our Father*; repeat steps 6 and 7 until all the Mysteries are completed **8**

Recite *Glory Be* and *Our Lady of Fatima Prayer* **7**

**11** Start of *Fifth Mystery*

Recite *Hail Mary* (10x) Try to meditate on the First Mystery as you pray **6**

Announce *First Mystery* and recite *Our Father* **5**

**12** Recite *Hail Holy Queen* and finish with the *Sign of the Cross*

Recite *Glory Be* **4**

Recite *Hail Mary* (3x) **3**

Recite *Our Father* **2**

**1** *Sign of the Cross* and recite *The Apostles' Creed*

## The Opening

With your fingers on the crucifix, pray the Apostles' Creed:

> I believe in God,
> the Father almighty,
> Creator of heaven and earth,
> and in Jesus Christ, his only Son, Our Lord,
> who was conceived by the Holy Spirit,
> born of the Virgin Mary,
> suffered under Pontius Pilate,
> was crucified, died, and was buried;
> he descended into hell;
> on the third day he rose again from the
>     dead;
> he ascended into heaven,
> and is seated at the right hand of God the
>     Father almighty;
> from there he will come to judge the living
>     and the dead.
> I believe in the Holy Spirit,
> the holy catholic Church,
> the communion of saints,
> the forgiveness of sins,
> the resurrection of the body,
> and life everlasting.
> Amen.

On the first large bead, pray the Our Father:

> Our Father, who art in heaven,
> hallowed be thy name;
> thy kingdom come,
> thy will be done
> on earth as it is in heaven.
> Give us this day our daily bread,
> and forgive us our trespasses,
> as we forgive those who trespass against us;
> and lead us not into temptation,
> but deliver us from evil.
> Amen.

On the next three small beads, meditate on the theological virtues of faith, hope, and charity while praying the Hail Mary:

> Hail, Mary, full of grace,
> the Lord is with thee.
> Blessed art thou among women,
> and blessed is the fruit of thy womb, Jesus.
> Holy Mary, Mother of God,
> pray for us sinners,
> now and at the hour of our death.
> Amen.

On the next large bead, pray the Glory Be:

> Glory be to the Father,
> and to the Son,
> and to the Holy Spirit,
> as it was in the beginning,
> is now,
> and ever shall be,
> world without end.
> Amen.

Pray the Fatima Prayer (there is no bead for this prayer):

> O my Jesus,
> forgive us our sins,
> save us from the fires of hell;
> lead all souls to heaven,
> especially those most in need
> of thy mercy.
> Amen.

## The Body

For each mystery and set of beads, pray in this order:
On the large bead, announce the mystery and pray one
Our Father.

On each of the ten small beads, pray one Hail Mary
while meditating on the mystery.

Pray one Glory Be and the Fatima Prayer at the end of the decade. (There is no bead for the Glory Be or Fatima Prayer.)

## *The Conclusion*

After the last mystery, pray the Salve Regina (also known as the Hail, Holy Queen):

> Hail, Holy Queen, Mother of Mercy,
> our life, our sweetness, and our hope.
> To thee do we cry,
> poor banished children of Eve.
> To thee do we send up our sighs,
> mourning and weeping in this valley of
>     tears.
> Turn then, most gracious advocate,
> thine eyes of mercy toward us,
> and after this our exile,
> show unto us the blessed fruit of thy womb,
>     Jesus.
> O clement, O loving,
> O sweet Virgin Mary.
> V. Pray for us, O holy Mother of God,
> R. That we may be made worthy of the
>     promises of Christ.

# Notes

1. Patrick Peyton, Father Peyton's observations on the Marian Document of Pope Paul VI, 08-02-03-12-00, Archives of Holy Cross Family Ministries, North Easton, MA.

2. Patrick Peyton, *All for Her: The Autobiography of Father Patrick Peyton,* ed. Wilfred Raymond (Notre Dame, IN: Ave Maria Press, 2019), 80.

3. Patrick Peyton, The Talk at Nazareth, May 24, 1971, 01-07, Archives of Holy Cross Family Ministries, North Easton, MA.

4. Patrick Peyton, Peyton's Journal, November 22, 1967, 09-17-01-17-00, Archives of Holy Cross Family Ministries, North Easton, MA.

5. Peyton, *All for Her*, 79.

6. Peyton, *All for Her*, 78.

7. Patrick Peyton, My Magnificat, 1990, 05-01-25-24-00, 6, Archives of Holy Cross Family Ministries, North Easton, MA.

8. Patrick Peyton, Material Requested by Father Pat for his book, –thoughts about my grandfather", Family Theater Papers, 09-17, Archives of Holy Cross Fathers Eastern Province, North Easton, MA.

9. John Paul II, "Pope John Paul II: Christ's Resurrection Was a Concrete Event," EWTN, accessed August 15, 2023, https://www.ewtn.com/catholicism/library/pope-john-paul-ii-christs-resurrection-was-a-concrete-event-158.

**Fr. Willy Raymond, CSC,** served as president of Holy Cross Family Ministries—an apostolate of the Congregation of Holy Cross, United States Province of Priests and Brothers—from 2014 to 2022. He continues to serve as an auxiliary priest in the Easton, Massachusetts, area.

Raymond joined Holy Cross in 1964 and was ordained to the priesthood in 1971. He earned a bachelor's degree in philosophy from Stonehill College in 1967 and a master's degree in theology from the University of Notre Dame in 1971.

Raymond served at Stonehill College (1979–1992), in Holy Cross leadership (1994–2000), and as national director of Family Theater Productions (2000–2014). He remains a diehard fan of the Boston Red Sox even though he served as chaplain for the Los Angeles Dodgers.

www.holycrossusa.org
www.fatherpeyton.org
Facebook: @wilfred.raymond.79
Instagram: @frwillyraymond
Twitter: @FrWilly

**Father Patrick Peyton CSC** (1909–1992), was a priest of the Congregation of Holy Cross who founded Family Rosary (1942) and Family Theater Productions (1947), which continue today under Holy Cross Family Ministries. He was a pioneer in using media for evangelization and produced more than eight hundred radio and television programs to inspire and educate families on the power of prayer and the Rosary. Peyton's cause for sainthood began in July 1997. He was declared venerable by Pope Francis in 2017.

# HOLY CROSS
# FAMILY MINISTRIES

At Holy Cross Family Ministries (HCFM), we believe
every family needs and deserves access to high-quality prayer
and faith experiences and resources. We are a mission-driven
family of Catholic ministries. Our mission is clear:
We are dedicated to inspiring, promoting and fostering
the prayer life and spiritual well-being of families throughout
the world. Families are served through faith-based video series,
prayer retreats, world-wide Rosary distribution, and numerous
interactive and in-person engaging prayer experiences!

## Our Ministries include:

- Catholic Mom
- Family Theater Productions
- Family Rosary
- Father Peyton Family Institutes in Peru and India
- The Peyton Institute for Domestic Church Life
  in the US
- Museum of Family Prayer

Visit **hcfm.org** to learn more.

# LEARN MORE ABOUT
# FATHER PATRICK PEYTON, CSC

This new edition of Peyton's biography tells the story of his life and dedication to the Blessed Mother as he discerned his vocation, overcame the obstacles of advanced tuberculosis and lack of education, and became a priest who eventually preached to more than 28 million people worldwide, worked with Hollywood stars, and founded Family Rosary and Family Theater Productions.